AF368091

you
+
me
=
love

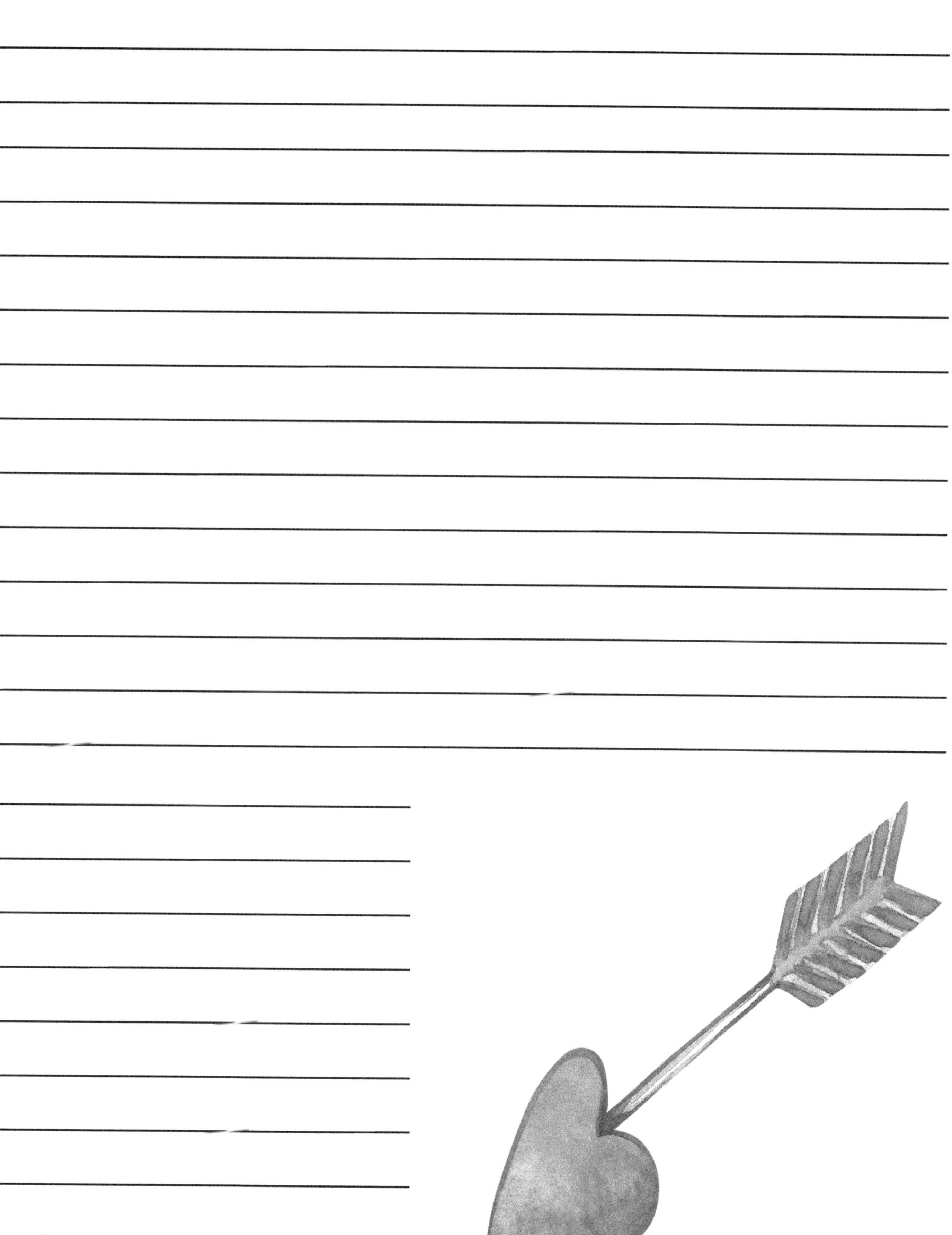

i love you

love you

you are loved

love
is all
you
need

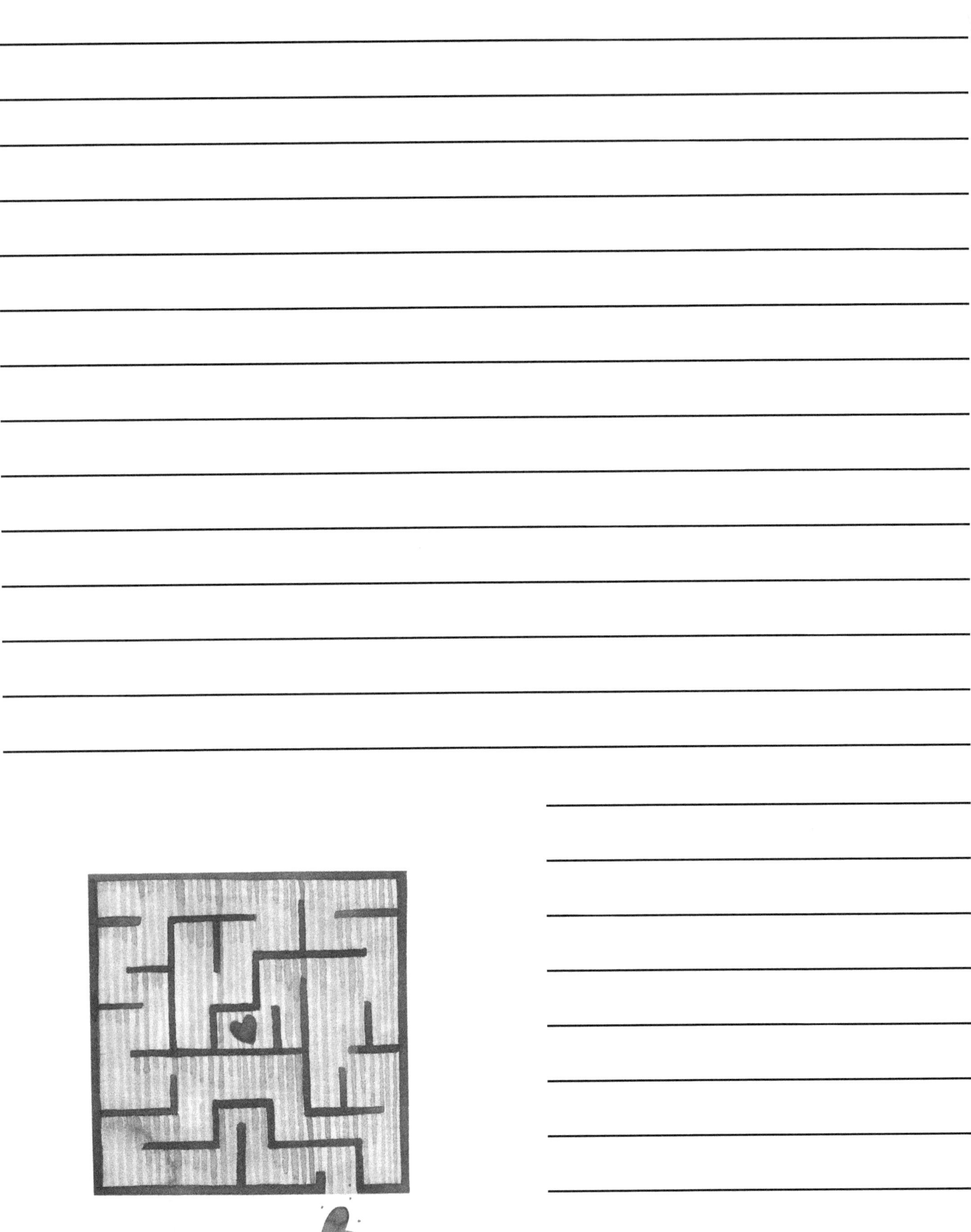

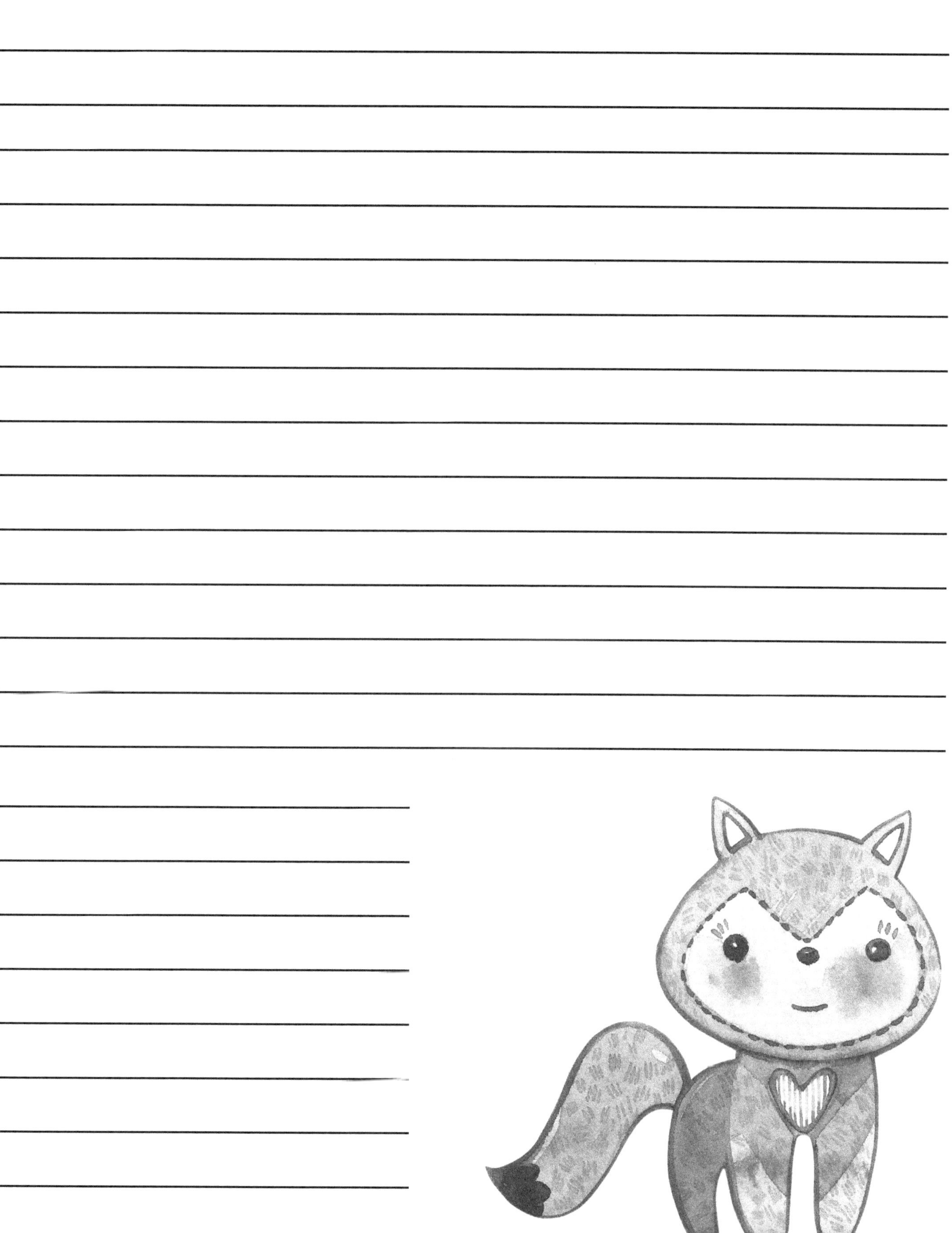

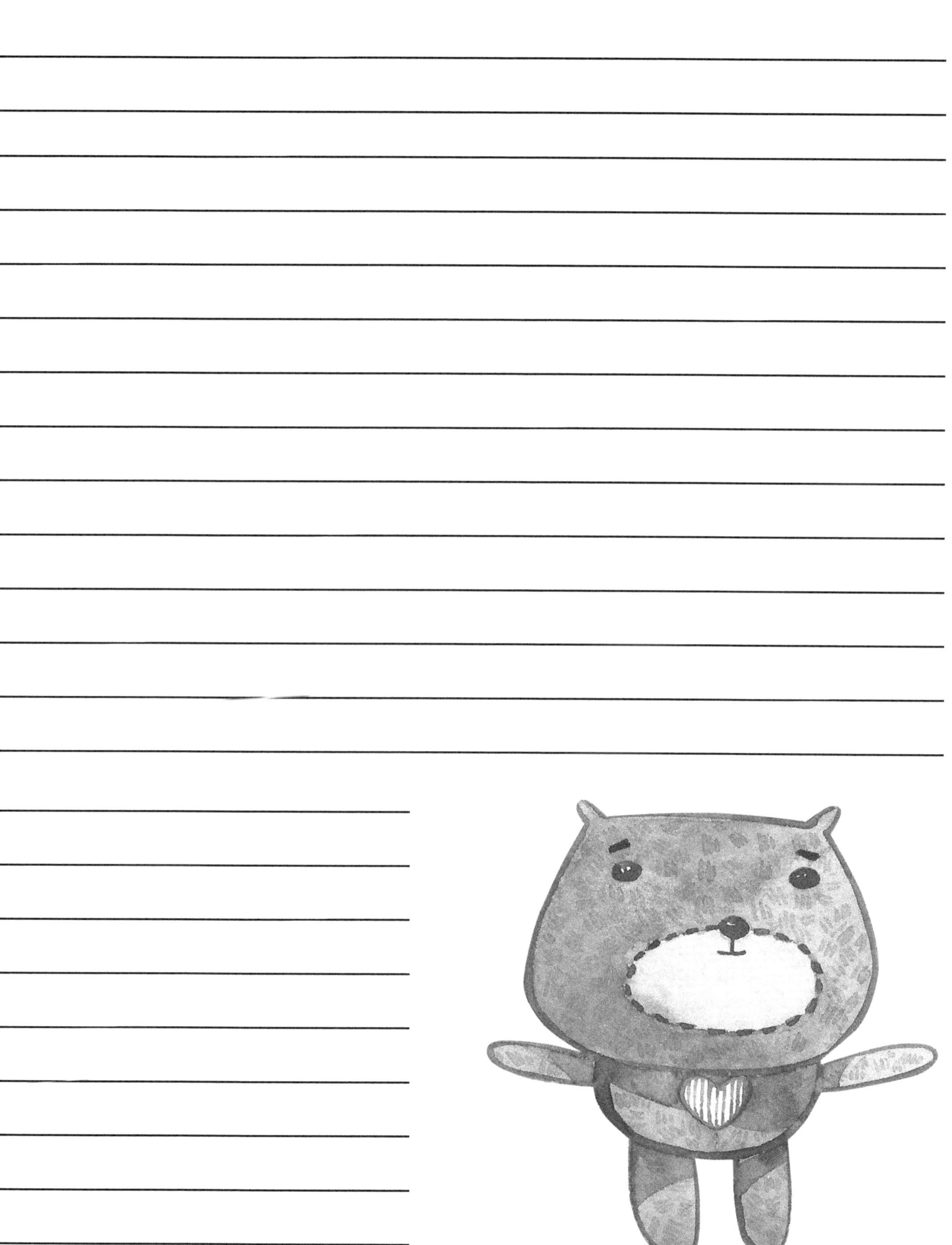

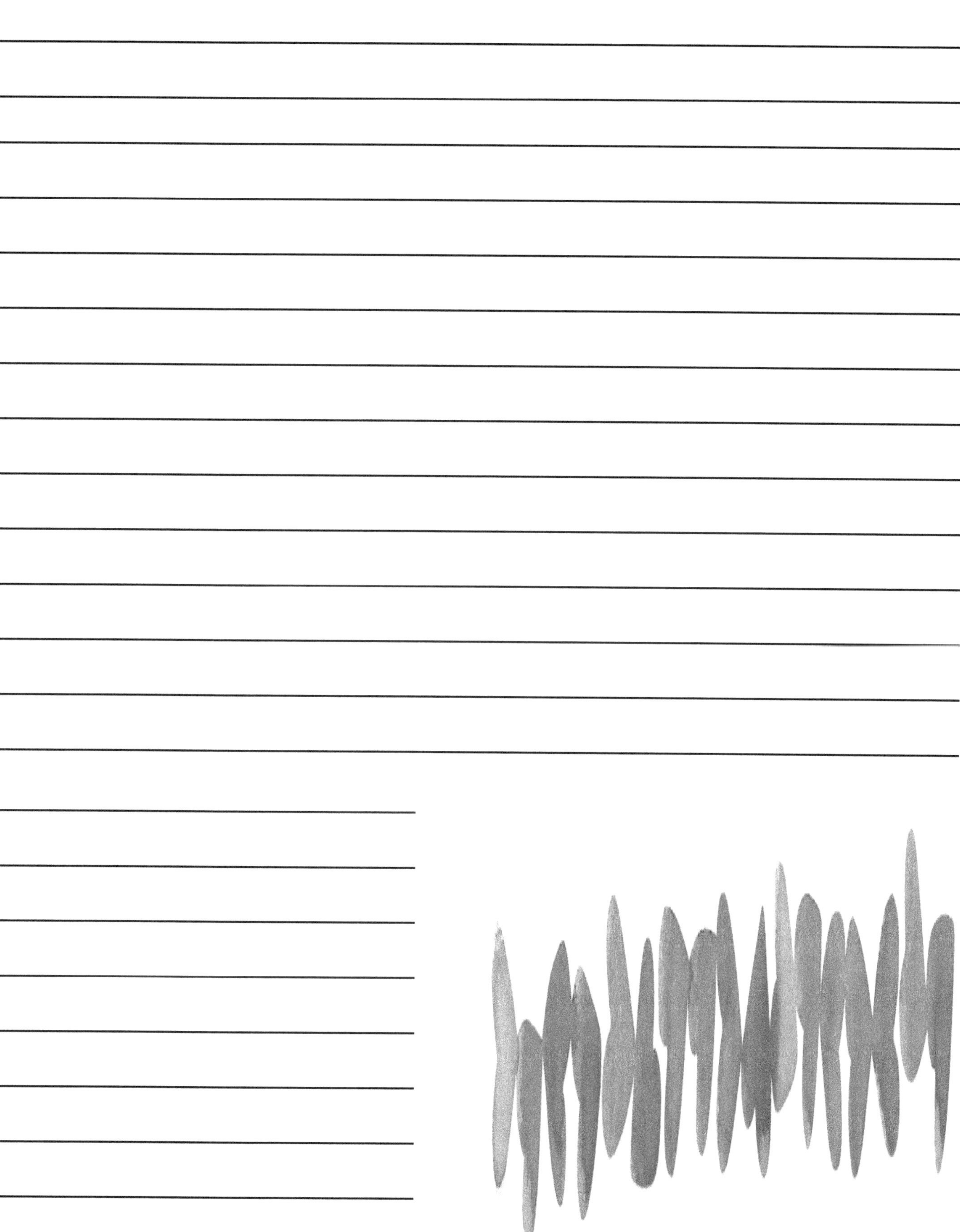

you + me = love

believe
IN
Love

i love
you

love you

you are
loved

love
is all
you
need

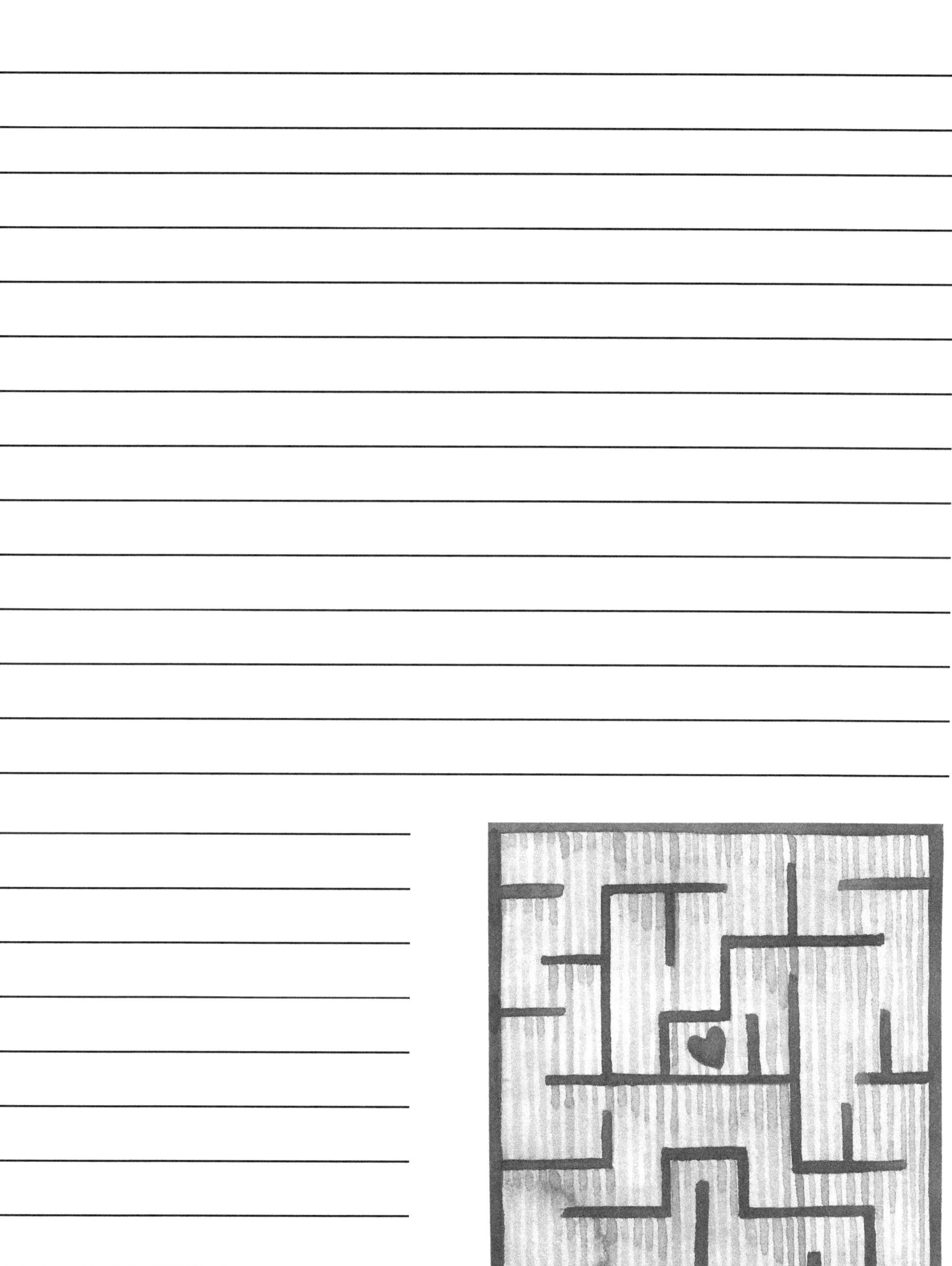

– Acts of Kindness Tracker –

- Acts of Kindness Tracker -

- Acts of Kindness Tracker -

Notes

Notes

Notes